THE VERGING CITIES

The Mountain West Poetry Series
Stephanie G'Schwind & Donald Revell, series editors

We Are Starved, by Joshua Kryah
The City She Was, by Carmen Giménez Smith
Upper Level Disturbances, by Kevin Goodan
The Two Standards, by Heather Winterer
Blue Heron, by Elizabeth Robinson
Hungry Moon, by Henrietta Goodman
The Logan Notebooks, by Rebecca Lindenberg
Songs, by Derek Henderson
The Verging Cities, by Natalie Scenters-Zapico

THE VERGING CITIES

poems

NATALIE SCENTERS-ZAPICO

The Center for Literary Publishing
Colorado State University

Copyright © 2015 by Natalie Scenters-Zapico.
All rights reserved.

For information about permission to reproduce
selections from this book, write to
The Center for Literary Publishing
attn: Permissions
9105 Campus Delivery, Colorado State University
Fort Collins, Colorado 80523-9105.

Printed in the United States of America.

Library of Congress Cataloging-in-Publication Data

Scenters-Zapico, Natalie.
[Poems. Selections]
The verging cities / Natalie Scenters-Zapico.
pages cm. — (Mountain west poetry series)

ISBN 978-1-885635-43-3 (paperback) — ISBN 978-1-885635-44-0 (electronic)
1. El Paso (Tex.)—Poetry. 2. Juárez (Chihuahua, Mexico)—Poetry. 3. Sister cities—Mexican-American Border Region—Poetry. I. Title.

PS3619.C285A6 2015

811'.6—dc23

2015002189

The paper used in this book meets the minimum requirements of the American National Standard for Information Sciences-Permanence of Paper for Printed Library Materials, ANSI Z39.48-1984.

Publication of this book was made possible by
a grant from the National Endowment for the Arts.

For my parents, who showed me how to fall in love with poetry,
and for Ángel, who I fell in love with in the verging cities
of Ciudad Juárez, Chihuahua, and El Paso, Texas.

CONTENTS

CON

Un cómplice perfecto. Un hermano gemelo. Hable de ser diferente, de descubrir algo importante. Algo por que pelear. Algo por que vivir. Lo que sea, una boca, una mirada, una mirada, un trato, un pacto: nunca separarnos.

A perfect accomplice. A twin. I talked about being different, about discovering something important. Something to fight for. Something to live for. Anything, a mouth, a look, a look, a deal, a pact: never split up.

—*Voy a Explotar / I'm Gonna Explode* (film 2008)

VERGE

CROSSING

Angel buys a passport made at a print shop for fifty dollars—perfect
but for a hair stuck in the laminate by his date of birth. *Not noticeable,*

he says and I believe him. We walk across the bridge to Ciudad Juárez
and I expect there to be an explosion—for the streets to glow red.

It's been five years since we've been back and the city is a ghost,
but the traffic is alive. *It's still a city,* I say. *Let's go to a bar,* he says.

We pose in faux fur with cigarettes for nightlife pictures, get vicious,
and leave at 3:00 a.m. I stumble in my platform heels and stop

at another bar to get drinks one last time in a to-go cup. By 3:30
I turn litterbug and throw our empties into the ink-stained street.

I brush my hands against the chain-link fence as we cross
the bridge back to El Paso. Cameras every ten feet—we smile

and kiss for them. Behind us a man yells, *That's it? That's all you have for me,*
murder capital of the world? Border agents wave us across—

I'm too white to tell and Angel looks clean enough, but one of us is illegal.
No one says a word—we all breathe pollution. To think we didn't need

to get a visa. To think we could have saved the fifty dollars. *Still easy,*
we laugh and agree to cross again next weekend. We wonder

why we call each other Cielo, why we call each other Angel? We wonder
how two cities are split, how they swell. Watch how they collide.

HOW BORDERS ARE BUILT

You lay me on blue sheets. I put two fingers in my mouth and they disappear.
In your hair a crown of border patrol point their guns at me; they watch
with night vision goggles to see if I'll wade across our river. I lick

the black corners of your ears; one agent shoots my shoulder. I wonder if you
could take them down while you're on top of me, put them in a box somewhere.
I tell you I am desert: my face cracks; reptiles hide in my shadows; my hair grows

because the wind pulls it. You push your face into my ear and I hear words
in dust storms. I cough as you push your shoulder into my mouth. My eyes
closed, I can feel the brush that grows along your arms reach for the sun.

You pull your face away and cry into my mouth. I can't drink all of you; tears spill
down my neck and across my body. I flood until you are swallowed too; grated
metal collapses into our streets; we pool around concrete tenements, land that never

holds a river quiet. We eat our border every hundred years then build it up again.
We ask each other if we've carried any foreign items today, barbed wire
fences stapled to our teeth, avocado pits in our back pocket. We say no.

BIBBED IN PAISLEY HE READS ŽIŽEK INSTEAD

of pulling September's steak tips from
a bag of peas in the freezer. On his lips

one hundred blue petals, dried flowers
from the bottom of a former lover's vase.

He licks his fingers, touches the hairs
of milled tree trunk in each page.

I wait; a flood runs from my mouth complete
with a rusted Honda Civic—the windows

all busted. My veins sprout to link my temples
to an electric socket. I black out and then

the most angelic resurgence of light . . .
He tells me I have become

an example of Žižek—*The unreal, we are*
fascinated by the unreal. I reach for my back

molar, turn it to the right and braid
my hair. *If I am unreal,* I whisper, *you must*

be as real as my hair, which I will cut
with these scissors. You tell me: *Cut it*

short. I've always wanted to know if I could make
love to a boy I've always known was a woman.

DEAR ANGEL,

There are days when the world is filled with numbers and we are bad at math. We eat breakfast in $f(x) = 2x$ and fuck in $d(5) = 76f + 86\pi$. These are days you become sick of guessing the moon's surface area. *I have no numbers,* you say. *I am named Angel in a sea of other Angels; how will you ever know to love me?*

And I say, *I'll call you the number 56; one day we'll learn to make love in differential equations.* You say, *I hate that number* and *I want to see objects in your face and see faces in the things you've left behind—I ask for such small pareidolia.*

I don't speak English well and I don't speak Spanish well and now I am illiterate. I will learn this lamp as I have learned your face—in grooves, shape, and gradation. They will say I am not a poet and I will know all the ways they've been scarred by the ring of their voices. I will sing, I will sing, I will sing—turned dumb, I will sing you dry.

I tell you to meet me at the point of a Mercator triangle at 7:00 but can't find you. Our earth is made of triangles that never measure 180°. What mathematical proof to run my hands along the rocks and let them drink of me. What lie to divide land in lines that don't exist, to attempt to leave the body on a dark, studded night.

You will go to the desert and there will be gull. You will run to the sea and there will be woodpecker. You will track these birds in the degrees by which they scatter and you will curl your body microscopic and I will hold you because you have no other language with which to understand.

You whispered late at night into your pillow and I heard this: *I hate letters as I hate numbers, as I hate nights you are gone. Come, memory, let me trace your eyes carefully. Let me learn you how.*

SUNDAY MORNINGS

While Angel watches *Antiques Roadshow*
I plant a hazelnut in his ear and watch its brown orb
take root inside him. I push it into his fertile brain

until leaves poke out of his teeth and red-bellied
woodpeckers eat his squirming veins. They steal

the black in his hair and make nests, eat his lips
and eyes, worms that crawl along his face. I too,
want to swallow his insides, but his smell reminds me

of my grandmother's closet. I run inside him,
wrap myself in old furs, and pick up shards of glass

from frames we broke the night I said: *I hate you.*
Under a fox hat is a box; inside are Angel's teeth.
I pull at each small pearl, and put them in a glass

to grow in milk. As each tooth grows roots, I string them
into a necklace. Angel appraises my art at 100,000 dollars

and tells me it doesn't matter, we can't travel anyway,
we crossed a desert eating tunas, and got pricked
with no papers. He draws an X on my hand

because he wants to marry me, only I am a dollhouse
he built of cardboard and soap. How he shook his hair

all over my body to dust me with the roughest snow,
snow we've only seen on TV outside *Antiques Roadshow,*
caught in the hair of women carrying fake Tiffany lamps.

THE CORNER STORE CLERK SAYS HER NAME WAS OFELIA

and it started with a phone call. A man
asking for 50,000 dollars. Ofelia
dressed her children in plain cotton. She rushed
them from store to car; parking lots are how

people go missing. The tree in her front yard
swollen with winged ants—she couldn't sleep.
Fear: the tree was dying. She forgot
to paint its trunk white. She plugged her ears,

disconnected the phone and boarded
every window. She dreamt her body cut
in half—a perfect border. When Ofelia
found her son's body on the lawn, a display

of limbs, she thought the word: rooted. His blood
was sap the tree could not stop oozing.

AFTER I READ YOUR OBITUARY

you crawl into bed with my husband
and me. Your body is smaller
than I remember. I hush your voice

when you complain: *The aloe vera*
in the pot is made of plastic.
Your breathing grows, a weed

in monsoon—you whisper: *Mother,*
father, and sister fell open as birds
in their chairs when they were shot

at dinner. You show me how
you dove under the table, felt specks
of their blood on your lips before

seeing the scuffs on your father's leather
shoes. As you measure the depth
of my weatherproof windows,

you tell me you buried your family
in the walls of an abandoned
restaurant. With the tip of the plastic

succulent I rub your swollen ears.
I tell you: *In this new country I am worse*
than the city of thousands dead;

I am a wound red with iodine. My husband
wakes and I beg him for water
I've never known to taste so clean.

PHOTOS FOUND ON A DEAD MAN'S PHONE

Image one: poinsettias, their leaves
dark stains on a tablecloth.

Image two: shirt collar wet
with sweat and air freshener.

Image three: all dark and then—

Image four: head of hair pillowed
by a ball of newspaper.

Image five: a face planted
in text—black stain on finger.

Image six: negatives in an envelope.

Image seven: electrical outlets, walls white
with scars—vines that grew too feral.

Image eight: opaque faces, their smiles
generic as a bar of soap.

Image nine: too much light, bodies
pressed through glass then left to wash in acid.

Image ten: exposed tongue—the buds missing.

Image eleven: flash, then the phrase—
our darkest corner damp with memory.

Image twelve: white sheets, a face
burnt orange in the light.

BECAUSE THEY LACK COUNTRY

1.

He goes to desert bars and searches every stranger's pocket
for the plastic heart, the stork that made him. He kisses

bathroom stall handles and eats the ice in the urinal.
Not México, not Canada, not United States, or the coat

made in Honduras, but the cloth of open sky
is what he wants. He is hungry as a bare flagpole

on a windy day. The streets moan when border patrol
finds him. He says: *Don't arrest me because I lack country.*

Plastic wrist ties, serial number, toothbrush, shampoo
in a plastic bag: he is made of what is missing.

2.

She hitchhikes down the freeway in a dust storm and covers
her ears as cars honk past—*qué mujer,* they holler.

The place where land and road meet, her body collapses.
Skin lifts to the sun in sheets, such thirst is only found

in those that cannot ask for water. She carries herself
to an abandoned outhouse; by night, border patrol finds her

with infrared scanners. They point their guns and the smell
of urine fills the room. *Filthy,* one agent spits to the earth.

They take her body in a paddy wagon and drive for days.
It doesn't matter the country—this desert is all the same.

3.

In bed she asks him: *Will you marry me?* He thought
she asked: *Can I give you country?*

His teeth are stars, and the stars are teeth,
and there is nothing to mark the difference.

He draws lines across her body in pen—openings
for respiration. He draws lines in squiggles, dots,

and mapped curves. He draws cursive that says:
our we, our we. The whole room dyed

red, he whispers: *Night vision goggles*
will always stain us—

ANGEL & I

fell asleep in an embassy while waiting for lines of red pen to run off a crisp linen page. i dreamt of falling on a jabón zote–scented blanket flocked with blue dust that breathes secrets telling me how to help angel get a paper that tastes like plastic & federal ink by getting married at twenty-one & eating the rice people threw at our wedding. i woke up in the same nappy chair that smells of valentina smeared over angel's passport photo & my eyes burning lashes and thoughts of green cards to a country neither one of us belongs in. an agent holding manila folders starts watching me through a glass cubicle watching me caress the face of a rubber stamp that had nothing to do with my loneliness & everything to do with angel's keys to a two-story home in oaxaca where a netted fence keeps out zapotec indians who are painting neon deer that will sit on a shelf in my laundry room.

in two years each deer will drink blue detergent when no one is looking.
in two years i will drink blue detergent when no one is looking.

in another three months our application will be up for review our marriage stuffed into a pillow sham & brought back to the factory that stitched it. i tell the agent angel's toothbrush is blue i sleep on the right side of the bed angel likes to eat mayonnaise with his steak angel can't make a fist because his hand was caught under a drill at a meat plant angel is not circumcised we sleep with the window open we don't take showers every day angel takes out the garbage on tuesdays. angel has fallen asleep again and the agent asks me to wake him. i tell the agent *he's dreaming*. the agent says angels don't dream. i wonder what angel dreamt of being when he was six because that i could never answer.

BROKEN INITIALS

JAM and BT and MB and UTB and NSZ and
your name: JOSÉ ANGEL MALDONADO.

We leak from the ear, the nose, the broken
tooth. We leak letters, small check mark:

NO tuberculosis. I found your ten-year-old
face under the laminate of the border crosser

visa. Unstamped passport, ITIN
on a loose sheet of paper, a signature that isn't

yours and isn't your mother's. A signature
of a man, the ink a black hole that swallows

each memory of light. Every book you've read:
gone, missing, gone. The dogtooth on each J:

gone. Wife's name: NATALIE SCENTERS-ZAPICO
DE MALDONADO, to show commitment.

Cashier's Check: 1500 dollars paid to
homeland security. Check: 600 dollars paid

to photocopy machine, typewriter, and
Bertha, who stamped each page

with an initial: JAM and BT and NSZ.
Bertha's Immigration: We Are Not A Legal Service.

IN A HALF-FULL BATHTUB

I hide a handheld mirror
between my legs to see

the wrinkled ridges—my half-
damaged erosion. No signs

of barbed wire, no men in green suits
with guns. I look for a shadow,

a haphazard line, a sign that you
were here once. At finding only myself,

I rest the mirror against the tile.
On the toilet, a bald immigration

official hands me paperwork
for the car, in your name,

I'll never see again. I plunge
the mirror back into the water

to see what reflection has made of me.
The man pulls the glass

from my hands, throws it against
the porcelain, and gently rubs the shards

across my face. Six weeks later—
a letter from my government:

it will take seven days for scar tissue
to arrive in a duct-taped box.

I LIGHT THE HOUSE ON FIRE AND LIE DOWN

on my kitchen floor to feel the ants search
the hidden sugars on my body. They are
a crown at my head. Above me, leaves

are suspended from the ceiling, leaves
that float up to the bare lightbulb that is
to them a moon. In my mind I solve the slope

between each ant and its corresponding leaf:
$m = (y_2 - y_1) / (x_2 - x_1)$. With the turn
of a compass I imagine your rise over run

a coordinate far away: a deer,
a raptor, an exoskeleton covered
in bright earth. The ants perform Mass

around me, and I remember:
the border agent, how he put his hand
on your head, how he lead you

to the car, how he arrested your body.
I want to think he blessed you
against the chemicals, the hose

they would spray you with. When
he called you *Illegal,* he asked
how I'd made love to an angel of other,

how our bodies had not shattered
in sin. I thought of how you could bring
quiet. But tonight the house glows

in fire. The ants form the contours
of your face—geography
of a body I cannot begin to measure.

NOTES ON CIUDAD JUÁREZ, AS A PLAY

Act 1: The strangers dressed in white sheets meet.
Scene 1: paint each other's hands blue.
Scene 2: feed each other clumps of powdered sugar.
Scene 3: light candles in four corners of a room.
Scene 4: sit on opposite ends of a table for three days.
Scene 5: eat baskets of fruit for the Assumption of Mary.

Act 2: The strangers fall in love.
Scene 1: climb over the table and cover each other's eyes.
Scene 2: scream when storms collapse their walls, light dies.
Scene 3: homeless, they walk through the aisles of the theatre.
Scene 4: they fall asleep, feet at each other's faces.

Act 3: The strangers are caught in war.
Scene 1: a foreigner promises rooms with electricity.
Scene 2: a foreigner undresses the strangers, wraps them in electric wires.
Scene 3: a foreigner kills one stranger; living stranger moves to a shantytown.

Act 4: Blackout on set.
Scene 1: a spotlight scans the apron for the living stranger.
Scene 2: the prompter loses twenty pages of script; exits through vomitory.
Scene 3: the spotlight is killed.

Act 5: The living stranger crosses a fence.
Scene 1: lights cued—living stranger opens mouth and finds a fence.
Scene 2: plucks fence from throat and bleeds for days.
Scene 3: plants fence and watches it grow for miles.
Scene 4: climbs through an opening cut with pliers.
Scene 5: with no money in a new land, her body is a thousand dimes.

THE VERGING CITIES WATCH ME

I walk home from a bar alone, stop
on Rim Road to let the lights of El Paso
and Ciudad Juárez switch on

and off, sew themselves over all the ugly
of my body. I hold my breath and hope
all that light will turn

into black beetles to swarm me quiet.
But when I open my body I am alone,
alone only the way these two cities can be

alone, only the way I am alone with him.
When we are naked, we are pale as fliers
for women gone missing. He whispers:

you'll never sleep at night if you don't look
at what I have hidden under my eyelids.
I inch the skin up like a blind, reveal two

nails where his eyes should be. If only
I had loved him sooner, how I'd have kissed
each eye green.

WHEN THE DESERT MADE US VISIBLE

You forgot to weed your eyes, so brush
has grown wild in your stare.

A wall of dust can travel miles,
blind us, choke us, stain us,
but not kill us.

Travelers think there's nothing in the desert;
they place themselves against
the bright mica and make it theirs.

They believe they are the first ones
to discover desert.

As though, in discovering desert, they could
populate it with trees
and dark mosses.

Because there are days the desert brings the sky
closer to my fingers,
closer to you—
I forgive the traveler.

You are the darkest places
of sparse and perfect language.

You are the darkest places
in the cloud's shadow.

DI VERGE

He didn't die, he grew so high alongside me that I can't reach him.

—*Anna Kamieńska,* A Nest of Quiet: A Notebook

SUCCULENCE

A wilted cabbage, collapsed, yawns
open, an abandoned accordion in
a red lit cantina. I forgot to water it
but I rip it free, the pot howling
with soil stuck in its molars, and I wash
the silt off with vinegar, eat the green
dinghies with croutons, tear its
bowels open with my teeth—
and at night its leaves cut me, its roots
shooting out of my ears and my fingers
and it sings of murder, all wildness.

IT'S THE HEAT THAT WAKES US

Five hundred feet away in Juárez, the maquilas
run all night. In El Paso, we share the same 110
degrees. Angel takes his clothes off and says:

The swamp cooler must be broken. Heat submerges
each building under an ocean thousands of years old.
Heat so thick I wonder what it is to be clean. I sweat

but Angel's lips are two ghosts rising to the surface
of his skin. He says: *I'm dying.* He says: *Mi amor,
you might be dead.* We don't touch; the heat

from each other's body is unbearable. I say:
I can't stop sweating. He says: *Become
the body of water to swallow us both.*

WOMAN FOUND NEAR SUNLAND PARK MALL

El Paso, Texas

When he finds the woman the Target customers
have been reporting, she is open-mouthed,

and whispers, *agua*. He thinks how common
to find a woman who crossed the desert without

enough water. He gets close to her face; her body
has betrayed her. Water is heavier the drier

the landscape. He puts his foot on her neck
and watches how slowly her face turns red with blood.

When the other border agents ask what state he found
this woman in, he has a story that involves water,

how some can buy it at Target and how others
don't know how to call it by its proper name.

A TORERO'S DAUGHTER IS KILLED

La Plaza de Toros, Ciudad Juárez

The bull runs through the gates, a tiny bride
on its back. Her gown flows bigger than her
body. The lace turns brown—trails through the arena.

Could the torero sing a melody to keep her
quiet, a melody to keep the crowd awake?

He thinks how beautiful the blood
would soak into the satin folds, how her hair
would come undone, become the rope to drag her.

He leans into his cape; the bull parades her,
his daughter, quinceañera, around the stadium.

He wants to carry her across the rose-covered dirt
into the desert, and then home. Knock down
a wall, place her in its empty and seal her inside.

He wants to see the white of her, feel her draw
circles with her eyes across his blood-strained neck.

He wants to know the pain his daughter felt
while still alive. Skull broken in the backseat
of a car, mouth open as a bull's eye.

LA MARISCAL CIUDAD JUÁREZ, MÉXICO

For Gloria Anzaldúa

She pushes her body against the brick, rubs her hands across
her shoulders, in circles around her breasts—licks her fingers
at men as they pass by. One has no money; he opens his mouth

and inside is an egg. He cracks it open with a knife. She thinks
of snakes, of nights when she peed the bed, afraid of snakes—
all the ones her mother warned her of. How they'd crawl inside her,

lay eggs, eat her body. He holds a knife to her throat; with two fingers
he pulls her cheeky curtain into a grin. He wonders when she ate so many
stars, how they stay hidden in the sky of her. Her blood drowns the city quiet.

PLACEMENT

1.

In the New York gallery the shoes hang by red ribbons. A storm
of high heels, of wedges, of flat sandals. This is for the women
gone missing. *This is tribute,* the artist says. *This is for awareness.*

2.

A book of poems about the women found in pieces. The line breaks, dis-
jointed like severed limbs across the page. I ask the author if she's ever been
to Juárez. She says, *It's terrible what's happening.* She doesn't face me.

3.

In the film, opera music bellows over photographs of women found
beheaded. The documentarian says she'll solve the mystery of the murders.
She says she only spent a year in Juárez and never returned.

4.

One poet says he doesn't know about the women but wrote
about the men—pacing the hotel lobby, talking about sand.
The border, he says, *I'll probably never go back.*

5.

Another poet says he keeps returning to the border. I tell him
I wish I had the same curse. He says, *It's hard to leave
the violence; some days I feel we never can.*

6.

The novelist says, *Hell must look like Juárez.* He says,
Bodies are buried in the walls of abandoned buildings.
But this violence wasn't enough, so he fictionalized it.

7.

I write of the boy I loved gone missing, his father found with no teeth
in an abandoned car. Some say you have no right to talk about the dead.
So I talk of them as living, their bodies standing in the street's bend.

A PLACE TO HIDE THE BODY

He is a boat beached in the desert, turning
black at the hull. He longs for an artificial lake.

A corroded can cut his foot, which hurts more
than where he's been shot, that gap

for his finger to fill. His blood is the bilge,
his heart the broken pump. I think he may

be dying. But in my ninth-grade history class
none of this is real because he is nowhere

in our film of Southwest culture. The documentary
says he wears faded polos and dress shoes two sizes

too big. The documentary says he never brings
enough water. But I know he wears the same

Aéropostale shirt as my brother and climbs
Mt. Cristo Rey every spring. When he's dead

they'll leave his body to the sun, an abandoned
ship in land the ocean's left behind.

GUERRERO PEARS

The tree hangs brown pears over his head.
From his pores white snakes pop. They swim
down his face to turn the soil. His tongue lies
in blood that's collected between his teeth.
He swallows red until he cries it. Streams run
around his nostrils; they bloom into a field
of roses at his chin. Birds perch on his gums
and drink the salt of him. His body, three feet
away in a cooler, rots with two beers and a knife.
His wide eyes are bruised and have turned black.
A girl comes to climb the tree for fruit and shakes
at each branch. The birds, scared, fly into the tree.
She opens the cooler, she covers her face, she
vomits. She looks at his head and says, *Un hombre.*

THE ARCHEOLOGIST CAME TO HUNT TRILOBITES

hidden in the rocks. He looked
for the curve of their antennae. He hunted
trilobites and ferns caked in white.

He hunted trilobites and ferns until
he found a human skull. A woman,
her teeth blanched yellow, her cartilage

slooped over her face. The archeologist
left her severed body for the sun
to eat, but then it wouldn't leave him.

He hunted trilobites and ferns, but after
that day, he left the desert and wrote:
The human skull was of a girl aged 16–22.

I'd never really seen violence
until that day. Her face was already
bone. Her body, scattered.

The archeologist learned how
to love a place quiet, pull it off you,
how to brush each bone and take

its print. The archeologist came to hunt
trilobites and ferns caked in white. Her remains
not worth burial or the glass case of a museum.

IN A DUST STORM

the paper is bleached quiet—
missing fliers caught
on the barbed wire rust

of the border fence—only some
make it to the cradled river. I catch
a flier in my hand—

a seventeen-year-old girl I knew,
her picture splotched with toner.
Her physical description reads

like an epitaph looking for its grave.
I let the paper fly again. I know
she is dead. I wonder when the wind will

stop, when it will rain again
to pulp this paper into something
solid. The desert in the afternoon

is haunting and these fliers
will never quit begging the brush
to stop their constant flight.

MOUTH IN MY KITCHEN

Mouth was split roja—my wound que no
curaba. Era mi boca, pero mi boca ya no hablaba.

Acaricié sus labios, esta boca opened itself,
two branches cut into a sky. *Mouth, it's true,*

I speak another language. Lips, the bumps
lodged along its tongue, I said:

Tell me I am lying. I stared at its cracked—
it was silent. I asked: *Mouth, are you dying?*

I asked: *Mouth, why have you come?* I asked
to fetch a dish. I asked: *Mouth, are you alien?*

Every time I creaked through the kitchen,
I told mouth it was stupid. Mouth:

pages from books it couldn't read.
I starved mouth, only to feed mouth

paper towels and mop water
over the sink. I told mouth: *Learn English.*

Mouth, like a child, pursed its lips and spat.
I asked: *Mouth, where is your body?*

I asked: *Mouth, where could your delicate hands be?*
Mouth floated above me, an uneven hole.

It would never leave me, this mouth. My id
mouth, this mouth—my mother's.

ANGEL REASSURES ME I HAVE ESCAPED THE VERGING CITIES

And when I realize that the woman in the film looks just like my sister and the film will end as all snuff films end, I wonder if I should turn off my computer.

And the lens, too burnt to tell if the man that pulls her hair has a cigarette or a toothpick in his mouth, only reveals I can't stand to see her planked body.

And when I tell myself the knife at her throat will kill her, I can't help but remember when I jumped into myself through a mirror at a bar where I had too much cocaine.

And how a blue-faced man put his hand up my skirt, how he delicately arched his fingers and made me cry until I thought: people find beauty in a field of weeds.

And the next day my mouth was an anthill and I cried in my closet thinking he'd be the only myrmecologist to see the colonies inside me.

And later I drank insecticide, but the ants poured out of my every orifice. They whispered: *Now we know your deepest tissue—it is rotting.*

And I asked: *Have I been rotting since they deported me?* And they said: *No, we've been boring holes in you much longer than that.*

And the weeds in my closet prophesized, before they died, that I'd be snapped in half and fed to monsters in an ocean I've never known.

And I know the weeds truly grow when I look closer at the screen and realize the girl in the film couldn't be my sister, but that braided hair could only belong to me.

A MASS GRAVE WASHED

with light from a moon
one year rising. Out of the earth

a thousand mouths surface, open
lipped and teething from the ground
that held them. A collection

of limbs all reaching for the cloud
that's come to sit so low the desert

chilled. Clothes are the first things
missing. An armpit: a mouth. A knee:
another mouth. The eye: a mouth

of teeth. The ear: a mouth of hair.
I am frightened of bodies dried

to bone. These once were people,
but I can't imagine them. These shoes:
not hers. These slacks: not his.

This shirt: not the child's or
the stranger girl's. The moon

continually rising, I wish it a death
only the sun could bring in rings of heat:
red, gelatinous, and boiled clean.

WHEN THE DESERT MADE US INVISIBLE

When I speak cactus falls
from of my mouth.

I cry as you pick up the thousand needles
fallen to our sheets.

Lately, there is such pain in speaking,
I think someone wants me quiet.

I think it's the travelers that want silence,
those who came to find themselves
in what they thought
were the desert's empty spaces.

I wouldn't trust this land
with existential questions.

The desert is the tumbled beauty of sky reflected
in a slender mirror of river.

I wouldn't trust the reflection
of shallow water.

Your thumb finds the last needles caught
at the back of my throat.

I choke at the sight
of blood on your fingers.

RE

Si el amor, como todo, es cuestión de palabras,
acercarme a tu cuerpo fue crear un idioma.

If love, like everything else, is a matter of words,
nearing myself to your body was to create a language.

—Luis García Montero, "El amor"

MERGE

EPITHALAMIA

1.

We married and my voice
became the park that held us.
A fertile ground that swallowed

each of my satin heels.
Your face became brass
in my hand. My hand,

dry wood across
your scalp. Your scalp,
a cabinet nailed shut.

2.

On our wedding night,
your body opened and closed,
a blinking eye—the pupil

dilated. Your mother told me,
watch for silhouettes. And because
I thought you were asleep

I moved your body to its side,
watched saliva form
a dark ring on your pillow.

3.

Your brother married
under a pillar of pink light—
his bride a face of weights.

Her dress tight
at the neck,
the lace a mouth

her chest was wearing.
A cross-stitched pull
for each smile.

4.

On his wedding night,
your brother fanned
his bride's white gown,

across a hotel bed.
His fingers, his new
gold ring, caught

at each button. Her body,
an open mouth. Under
her tongue, the pearl missing.

5.

Your sister married
a soldier. His eyes,
two shadows dancing

alone down the longest
hallway. Your mother
opened her front door

and his awkward figure stood
in the brightest spot, his mouth
trembling for more light.

6.

On her wedding night,
your sister couldn't sleep.
She searched the room

for food, hungry
for the bird she saw
just after the ceremony.

Her husband slept,
as he did at dinner,
his eyes red-open.

7.

Our children will call this
the season of weddings.
A wedding followed

by an interview. A wedding,
a dark fingerprint, a green card
hard enough to pick a lock with.

A wedding to the slow snaps
of the camera. Your brother, your
sister, your mouth, a wet star drowning.

VERGE

1. a. The male organ; the penis.
   b. *Zool.* [After modern French use.] The male organ of a mollusc, crustacean, or other invertebrate.

3. A species of torch or candle. *Obs. rare.*

4. a. A rod or wand carried as an emblem of authority or symbol of office; a staff of office; a warder, sceptre, mace.

6. An accent-mark. *Obs.*

14. a. The extreme edge, margin, or bound *of* a surface of an extensive nature, but regarded as having definite limits.
    b. *fig.* The end *of* life.

17. a. The brink or border *of* something towards which there is progress or tendency (from without); the point at which something begins.

—*Oxford English Dictionary*

ANGELS FALL FROM THE SKY TO EL PASO, TEXAS

I wonder what he sees first: a building,
perhaps a bank of windows cutting
into the sky. Or a road, a freeway stitched
with cars so small it looks like a fine

embroidered curtain. And Angel,
what do you think of? Do you think:
This is me—dying in the sky? Do you
scream to God? Do you tell him,

you are not that kind of Angel? Do you say:
I am merely a man named Angel—
I have no wings to fly. And when he does not
listen, do you scream or close your eyes

and unwrap the gift of gravity? That pull,
that tug of organs. And Angel,
do you see me? Just before you hit
the middle of five o'clock traffic?

Running on the sidewalk searching
each body as they hit the ground
for any one of them that might be you?
A city of fallen angels, each one a collection

of human arms and legs, a torso, and
bleeding mouth. I knew when immigration
arrested you, when I had to pay a fine
for ever having loved you, that they would

take our one bedroom, our washer and dryer—
anything of value. But how was I to know
that even God would push your frail form
from the sky? So when I find

your body naked, your skull cracked
in shards across the tar, I take
my clothes off and cover you.
You whisper: *I can't die here, I wanted*

to fall on the live side of the border.
And I know it isn't your voice
I'm hearing but I take your severed hands
and carry them across to Juárez anyway.

I breathe bone as I cross—your blood running
to my elbows. I breathe. I breathe
to exchange your body for an explanation.
I breathe. No one says a word; I breathe.

THE CITY IS A BODY SWALLOWED

We align our backs until we share
the same spine. Your vertebrae

are the numbered metal poles
that mark this part of the border:

357, 358, 359. You are the twin
I swallowed lost within

a mother's womb. I thought
you'd died, but look how deep

you fell inside me. A ball
of teeth and hair nestled

in my throat. When I speak
no one remembers how shallow

our river can be, an arm cut
from the body of its meaning.

A JOURNALIST'S FIELD NOTES ON THE KENTUCKY CLUB
Ciudad Juárez, México

At 7:30 p.m. the bar is at capacity. Have I ordered the wrong drink? Many businessmen in suits order cheladas with lots of lime and salt in frosted glasses.

Their suits are dark, I wonder if they are actually shadows.

People make jokes about studying at Conalep, trade school alternatives to high school, that are classist and vague. I need to visit a colonia called Anapra next. The word Anapra has no origin, as though its linguistic roots don't belong to the living.

At 9:00 p.m. a Mexican man approaches me and asks in perfect English where I am from. I make small talk and tell him Minnesota. He says if I've come to get drunk at the Kentucky Club I'm doing a bad job. He leaves, laughing quietly out the door. I wonder how much it's snowed back home, and I'm surprised by the wind here.

I learn from the bartender that Marilyn Monroe and Frank Sinatra were regulars at the Kentucky Club. I ask if anyone working tonight remembers them coming in. He says no one in Juárez remembers anything. I wonder if he didn't understand me.

Then military boys order tequila. They joke about how the internet is still a myth in Anapra and how the girls there are sluts.

They say you don't have to buy a prostitute when you can go to Anapra and pick up a fifteen-year-old for free.

They say, sometimes these girls' grandmothers will let you in at night. And if you're a jotito, then there's plenty for you too, they say, pointing at one of their friends, laughing.

I leave the bar by 10:00 p.m. The streets are lined in bags of sand in case of late-night crossfire. I walk the street and wonder if someone shot me right now, what part of my body would be hit and if I'd survive.

I see people walking but no one smiles and I am not met by any guns, knives, or other weapons.

When I open the door to my hotel room at 10:15 p.m. I am disappointed that nothing more violent has happened. The streets are only shadows cast by figures, and not shadows of the dead.

GIRL CURLED OVER A BAR STOOL

At the club she tells me she doesn't accept
cash anymore. Only stamps like the ones
she has over her nails, the ones that flicker
when she moves. I think her body a package
I could send to anyone in the room. She says,
You've forgotten I'm naked. She says, *I'm waiting*
for you to kiss me. She says, *You're useless.*
Only I can't touch her. Her mouth broken
at each side with yellow pus disgusts me.
I think she's diseased and I don't want to help her.
I hand her twenty dollars to leave me alone
and she does. I wonder when she'll notice
the blood caught in the grooves of that bill.

THE VERGING CITIES

1.

Our river has long dried but I can still see
the vapors of your body rising. I am the city

with high-rise buildings between my legs.
Your eyes are tiny glass windows glittering.

Do you remember nights we rolled together
in the currents of white streets? Those were nights

a stench would wake me, and I could never tell
if it was your sewage or mine. Those were nights

I dreamed your body a verge marked in deep lines—
border of our extremities.

2.

I am the city that's come to swallow
the plastic bags of your body. I have seen

you sit in parking lots, whispering of light
and the smoke that rises from me.

Because you think me a woman, you think me
beautiful, but we are of the same concrete.

At night I grow hysterical and scream:
open your home, open your home to me.

You drive our children to desolate places
and pretend they aren't yours.

3.

I walk through the concrete cradles built to channel
our century flood. We mark the world in lines

and forget the land never knew them. Watch
the drywall houses in the arroyo get washed to rubble.

Our verge is the male organ of a mollusk trapped
in sediment. Our children's origin lies in the mollusk,

in the mountain once submerged, in the presence
of our bodies. Some nights a child's scar is beautiful

and some nights a child's scar is a single candle burning
a house made with tin to the ground.

4.

You turn on every bulb, make it flower
light and wake me. The night you bathed

our children in gasoline, took pictures of them
nude, and burned their shoes, I decided

I would never forgive you. That night,
with a gas mask on, you greeted me

and I could not understand why you denied it,
even after the photos developed. When it rains,

the ping, ping, ping on your roof makes me wonder
how I've ever been able to sleep next to you.

5.

Longing brings me to your door. I hide my face
in smog because I know that still excites you. Your hands

leave broken bottles and receipts behind my ears.
A border agent at the foot of the bed, we clean the dirt

from each other's body with our tongues—you want
to humiliate me. We enter each other with no moisture,

ooze only silt. After, you cry when the roads we have graveled,
the fences you have built, return and keep us from

each other again. This is how you degrade me, your sister,
your lover. This is how you degrade yourself.

THE CITY IS A BODY BROKEN

Most days, the light falls so thick
I don't know what it is to be
without it. At night we lie

in bed away from each other,
the moon so bright it is a scrim
for the sun. When clouds come,

monsoons flood freeways, trap
old tires against barbed wire.
Your body, a victim of erosion,

turns bone. I jump from our chain-
link bridge and only break a foot.
Which of us has become

the natural disaster? In bed, I blame
the fever, the sores that line my mouth.
But it's my foot that's swollen. I wrap

it in custom's forms. Will I ever know
where you hide my money, or
the mountains where I hide your guns?

IN THE MORNING I FEEL ANGEL'S BREATH

on my barren places. The weathermen
and almanacs got it wrong—it didn't rain
all July and my skin flakes and peels
for him. My nightgown pushed
to my chest in sleep, I only want
to be inundated. Angel asks about the boy
who loved me first and I tell him how
I bled until my body felt familiar and foreign,
like the country the boy had taken me to—
an open wound I would desire all my life.

BECAUSE YOU DON'T HAVE A SOCIAL SECURITY NUMBER

I weave slips of paper through the grated metal
at spot 357. Each slip is a letter, a watercolor, a kiss
on a white wall, a memory of the house you hung

stars in. I write so you'll remember the cacti—
how to draw them on my chest, cacti that bloom into tunas
that turn our fists red. I write you an apology, words that bleed

into pictures of the day I screamed: *357-89-0861*. I write:
You couldn't hear me because of the water—the way they hosed
you down like cattle. 357-89-0861, you can keep it, it was mine—

I've learned to hate this number. I can't remember
why we never married, why I was so afraid
you would plant a desert in my chest and thirst for it.

I write: *Come meet me at spot 357; we can water*
the only tree to grow along this border, kiss through
the diamond mouth of a metal fence. I pray

these slips of paper reach you, that they don't become
the ragged shirts lost in storms. Let me wash
your face in numbered sections and call you husband.

And when border agents come, may people say we made
this fence our home, pushed our faces into its links,
and let the rocks bury our bodies—*357-89-0861*.

ANGEL AND I ARE BOTH GREAT PRETENDERS,

riddled at night by seizures—Phenobarbital,
our cheap anticonvulsive. They tell us

Juárez is not a war and Angel cries at night
thinking of his father unsafe in his house forever.

We can't sleep, so down to the carpet, a new position.
No pillows, only thoughts of frozen fish fertilizing

the tomato plants, thoughts of bulls disappeared
from their pastures, thoughts of fingers hidden

in the glove box. Angel cries so I use my wedding band
to collect his tears, but hollow rings hold nothing.

He cries and I think of us as stars, until stars
become too sentimental. At night we force

our bodies to lace together and fall apart,
desperate vines searching for any wall.

LIKE VICTORIAN WOMEN

the dogs are sick with malaise. They lounge in the street
to cure their deep ennui. Sheets billow on clotheslines
like distant sails darting the horizon. Angel photographs

strays in every restaurant and store. This is how
we remember home: dogs howling deep, then
in high falsetto. On long walks Angel chases

after every dog, calling: *Judas, come here, Judas.*
He imagines them as forgiven traitors. Angel says
sometimes the boy in him goes missing. He becomes

a dog in the lurch, sharp with teeth. *Some days a dog*
is seldom, he says. *Some days a dog is hardly seen.*
I ask what he means and he shows me our wedding photos,

in the background a stranger holding a panting dog. *Strange,*
only one dog came to our wedding, he says.
The dog's tongue a flooded canyon—dried, then gone.

YOUR MOUTH IS FULL

of prickly-pear jam, goat cheese, and cracker.
As you speak, your gums might be bleeding,
I can never tell from the shadow. I laugh at how
you call each card: *Con los cantos de sirena,*

no te vayas a marear, el farol de los enamorados,
cuánto apache sin huarache. Each black bean
dances across our uneven table, so neither one of us
can tell who is winning. You pull el cotorro

from the deck and I confess, *My wedding dress,*
I found it full of cocoons. I sent the dress back home
with my mother. As you shuffle the deck, you say,
Your mother's verging cities must be hungry then;

since they couldn't have you for a wedding,
look how they took the dress instead. We laugh
and dance each time another bean strikes
four across the board. I've almost won

but am missing el cornudo. I tell you, *My dress,*
my poor dress, what will the verging cities do to it?
Your mouth full and red, you say, *They'll cry*
for your white dress until one city wears it, and the other

can tear at it from behind. One sister, beautiful,
the other, hysterical for the moon behind the sun.
You call: *El que te mata.* I say: *Lotería,*
el diablo o la muerte? You say: *No, el alacrán.*

THE SUN THAT TENDS TO FIELDS OF GRAIN BURNS

the brush brown this time of year. Smog hangs
over the sister cities like a horde of angels
so thick I open my mouth and bumps appear

on the tip of my tongue. From the freeway, I see
the cemetery where my body will one day rest.
When I'm dead the rush of cars will be a sea

of frothing waves. The earth's strata will be the weight
of water I've never known. Its weight will pull
at my uterus, sit on the square jaw of my face.

I will never taste the rocks, the seeds, the dirt
in this air again. A handkerchief balled at the back
of my throat, I will suffocate if ever I stir awake.

The devil will pluck my tongue and press it between
his jaws. He'll tell me: *Your body once was ocean*
that the desert, in its thirst, swallowed whole one night.

ENDNOTES ON CIUDAD JUÁREZ

1. The larger portion of this text discusses El Paso, Texas, the boring sister to Ciudad Juárez, México.

2. There are apartments that feel like they are by the sea, but out the window there is only freeway.

3. The geraniums always wilt either from heat or pollution.

4. El Canelo is the red-headed Mexican boxer who speaks Spanish.

5. Sometimes the candles are religious, sometimes they are not.

6. The girl from Juárez is beautiful. The girl from Juárez is God.

7. The tortilla border has shanties on one side and trailers on the other.

8. Some call them Fronchis because their license plates read: Fron-Chi for Frontera Chihuahua. Some just call them fresas.

9. In summer, roaches cross the street and travel home to home like people.

10. Campestre, Anapra, Chaveña, Anáhuac, Flores Magón, and Independencia are only some of the neighborhoods in Ciudad Juárez.

11. Some streets are lined in wires because it's so easy to steal electricity.

12. Moxas graffiti walls: *mee aamooo!! noo aa laas coopiioonaas!!*

13. Some days saliva evaporates from the tongue.

14. The river has become the only blue vein left pulsing on the map.

15. The river is only blue on the map.

HOW BORDERS COLLAPSE

Ofelia and Luis, Mauri and Sofia,
line their cars at the border wall
and stick their fingers through

its rust mouths. Sugar deep
in the crevices of their hands,
the dead come to meet them.

Not as translucent ghosts, but alive.
They park their cars in the U.S.
and México, their arms full

of sunflower seeds, full of new
beginnings. Even Angel's grandfather
has come to tell stories of how

he died on the wrong side of the border.
He wants us to understand why he stayed
in the U.S. alive, and how he hates

this city's Christmas-lit star and how
he'd prefer the white rocks of its sister.
He says, the cities have become

so bright the dead can't sleep
their eight hours. He says, the cities
are verging again and soon no one

will tell the difference between the shanties
of this colonia and the iron gates
of that neighborhood. He puts a finger

in each ear; the noise of the living
is bothersome. This morning
everyone in the cities is alive again.

Their eyes open to the sun,
their fingers collapsing
chain, link by link.

ACKNOWLEDGMENTS

Many thanks to the editors of the following publications, where some of these poems first appeared, some in earlier forms:

American Poets, the *Believer, Prairie Schooner, West Branch, Crab Orchard Review*, the *Massachusetts Review, Four Way Review, As/Us, Palabra, Cura, Cream City Review*, the *Minnesota Review, Bellevue Literary Review*, and the *Acentos Review.*

"Endnotes on Ciudad Juárez" was selected by Sherman Alexie for *The Best American Poetry 2015*.

Special thanks to my mentors in Albuquerque, New Mexico: Lisa D. Chávez, Dana Levin, Luci Tapahonso, Greg Martin, and Jesse Alemán. I would also like to thank those who first encouraged me to write in El Paso, Texas: Benjamin Alire Saénz, Sasha Pimentel, Daniel Chacón, Jeff Sirkin, and Arturo Ramos.

Bonnie Arning, Nora Hickey, and Nick DePascal, thanks for growing with me as writers. Nic Smith and Erik O'Brien, thank you for making me feel welcome in your city when I was missing mine so much.

Thank you, Mom, Dad, Ethan, Elaine, and Grandma, for always letting me pursue poetry without question. Gracias, abuelita y abuelito, por siempre hablar español conmigo desde mi niñez. Ángel, mi amor, thank you.

And thank you to Stephanie G'Schwind, Donald Revell, and everyone at the Center for Literary Publishing for giving this book such great attention.

This book is set in Sabon
by The Center for Literary Publishing
at Colorado State University.

Copyediting by Karen Montgomery Moore.
Proofreading by Cedar Brant.
Book design and typesetting by Katie Naughton.
Cover design by Melissa Hohl.
Printing by BookMobile.